BAGSY THAT

BAGSY THAT

Bagsy That

…and other Christmas poems

Stephen Williams

CONTENTS

BAGSY THAT

Solstice Poem

Now the summer's over and the earth's begun its turn
And the sun's thought better of it and we've had our chance to burn
And the factor 30's shelved and your bikini's had its day,
Do the one thing that will chase those painful summer blues away.

You may think it's too early, but please take a different view:
Remember, someone should be first so it may as well be you.
So fetch the ladder from the shed with no more hesitations
And climb into the attic for the Christmas decorations.

In the Foyer

Bunking off maths, decorating the tree,
In the foyer at Christmas, Amy and me.
Baubles and fairy lights strewn on the floor,
Boxes and plastic bags blocking the door.
Teachers walk onwards with glances approving;
Time's ticking over, but we're not for moving.
Tied up in tinsel, defying the bell -
If we string this thing out,
We'll miss science as well.

Are You Hanging Up Your Stocking?

In among the mince pies wander;
Over tills, a guiding star.
Celebrations tins stacked yonder;
Nuts and dates and blah blah blah.
Cliff and Slade and Wizzard jingle,
Jaded shoppers intermingle
Worlds away from winter's tingle -
End of August in the Spar.

Christmas Eve Steve

He sat and drank our coffee as the clock ticked round to three.
And helped himself to six more chocolate snowmen off our tree.
He'd never been a brother that was ruled by tide or time,
But believe me, Steve, on Christmas Eve, he liked to cut it fine.

His coat had hung for hours and his shoes sat by the fire;
But Steve, like every Christmas Eve, was showing no desire
To catch the bus and scoot round town for presents for the
                                                morning;
He was happy with his feet up, cracking monkey nuts and yawning.

But then, at four, the moment that we couldn't quite believe:
Our horizontal Steve on Christmas Eve began to leave.
He pulled his hat down low and wrapped his scarf around his chin.
And stepped into the street, his Christmas shopping to begin.

And though the shutters on the stores were straining at each hinge,
A million dads and Steve were on their yearly retail binge.
A thousand miles an hour through rain to Debenham's and Next;
Poundland queues of lots more dads, defeated and perplexed.

Through underwear in Marks and round to Smith's for pads and
                                                pens;
At ten to five our man had bagged the relatives and friends.
And hark the herald angels sing, some packages from Ste!
Are wrapped and bowed and waiting underneath our Christmas
                                                tree.

When morning comes, the kids attack the boxes with real joy:
A book from aunty Vicky and from uncle Mark, a toy.
And Steve? Was there a consequence for being glib and sluggish?
Well yes, 'cos this year, just like last, he'd bought a load of rubbish.

Nativity

My son, aged eight, came home from school
One cold December day.
Bless his heart, he'd got a part
In this year's Nativity play.

"A tea-towelled shepherd? The leading man?
Tell me son and tell me now. "
And after three he said to me:
"I'm going to be a cow."

"What was that?" - my short reply.
"Did I just hear you right?"
"Yes," he said, and bowed his head,
As all my nerves got tight.

"A flippin' cow!" I blurted out.
"You must be having me on.
I'll tell you flat, I'm not having that.
Now pull the udder one. "

He hardly stood out Christmas last
And we could barely see
Behind his class, as he read as
'Narrator 23'.

He'd seen me burn like this before;
He rolled his eyes at me:
"Leave it dad. It's not so bad
At least I'm not a tree. "

"Tree beats cow any day son.
You can sway in the blowing wind."
I got up from my chair and showed him right there,
And he stared at me and grinned.

BAGSY THAT

"A cow just moos like a cow does best,"
I said with a know-it-all tone.
You're no farmyard beast!" My rage increased.
"Now where's that bloomin' phone?"

"Leave it, Dad! Don't phone Mrs Jones
This part for me will do."
He closed the doors, got on all fours
And performed a brilliant moo.

I will admit, I was impressed
Although it was bizarre.
But when he said he'd sleep in the shed,
I thought that was going too far.

So, I phoned her up and bent her ear:
"What are you playing at?
He's a clever lad; you must be mad
To give him a part like that."

She listened, or I think she did,
And then she said to me:
"No change of heart; he's got his part.
At least he's not a tree".

I said, "Don't start that. I've just been there.
Look, can't he be a king?
He's got a crown; I'll send it round,
He's good with rules and things."

Waste of time, so I just hung up -
A bit abrupt, maybe.
Just because, it really was
Like talking to a tree.

So showtime came; the lights grew dim.
The parents sat upright.
Speech from Jones: "Switch off your phones.
And please enjoy the night".

And there he was: the cow's front end.
His mate Joe at the rear.
Trotting along, singing a song.
I couldn't help but cheer.

The whole production - what a thrill
The children were sublime.
Funny things like rapping kings -
It was more like a pantomime!

Dancing sheep and Elvis shepherds
Swaying trees - like I said
All to please us, even baby Jesus
Was a Barbie without a head.

At the end we stood and clapped
Until our hands were aching.
The show was closed, then they all posed
While photographs were taken.

And while the parents chatted on,
Showing pictures on their phones,
I broke free and took my tea
And went straight for Mrs Jones.

Sheepishly, I shook her hand
And looked her in the eye.
I was contrite, said she was right
And dribbled down my tie.

BAGSY THAT

"Mrs Jones, your casting's great;
With that I won't contend.
You were right to say my lad could play
A perfect cow's front end.

But next Christmas, don't you think he could,
Depending on the show..."
I didn't dwell, as I could tell
She wanted me to go.

So if your child comes home with news
That makes you quite irate,
Avoid a quarrel and hear the moral
That I will now relate.

When your kids are only picked
As bit-part farmyard creatures,
Don't be a fool; just play it cool -
And always trust the teachers.

Santa Special

We're on the Santa Special.
We're rolling down the track.
The big guy's in our carriage
Handing presents from his sack.

We've had some mince pies, Coke and sweets,
Tons of Christmas cheer.
We adore the Santa Special
And might bring the kids next year.

Top of the Tree

She's got to have the best tree
My mum at Christmas time.
She's planned it since July -
Her reputation's on the line.
But this time she's gone way too far;
She doesn't know where to stop.
In her quest to beat the neighbours,
She's put my sister on top.

Handmade

Here come the baubles; here come the scenes.
Here come the golds and the silvers and greens.
Here come the robins on snowy spade handles.
Here come the skaters and clusters of candles.
Here comes a funny cartoon of an elf.
But this card to you, I created myself.

It all started well; I found all my pens
And scissors and Pritt stick, a few odds and ends.
I settled myself by the fire with a brew
And felt quite inspired with the tree that I drew.
But gradually I could see things were not right;
The Christmas card art world it wouldn't excite.
My green felt tip pen started losing its ink
So I scraped it too hard and I just didn't think.
I started to panic; my mind was unstable.
I went through the card and ruined the table.

BAGSY THAT

But as I was sponging and rubbing the mark,
The dog took the card and ran down to the park
So I had to give chase down the road in the rain
In my slippers, but as I'm not one to complain,
I just sprinted on, caught up with the mutt
And wrestled your card and straightened it but
It was looking a state with the creases and that
And I tried all I could, but it wouldn't go flat.

Now the burn in the corner, well this is the thing:
Some carollers came and, well, started to sing.
My progress was good; it was under the iron
(I was pressing it hard while my slippers were drying).
But as they struck up with Away in a Manger,
I left the hot iron stuck fast to the paper.
I threw them a pound and ran back to the kitchen

And stared as the flames round the room began twitching.
But soon the whole house was full of black smoke
So I grabbed your card quick as I started to choke.
As I ran to the street to watch the inferno,
The engines arrived, but I wasn't concerned though
'Cos safe in my hand, and I didn't feel bitter,
Was the unfinished card in need of some glitter.

Now the bullet hole on the left side near the tree,
Has an interesting story attached to it, see:
On the way to the Spar for the glitter I mentioned
This kid with a shotgun, had one clear intention.
He pointed the thing and demanded my cash.
So I showed him your card all covered in ash
And I tried to explain, but he thought me a bore.
So he fired the gun and I dived to the floor.
I imagined I'd fallen into an abyss,
And I thought to myself: I've got to tweet this.
I didn't get hit, but the card sadly did.
And the robber got off with a couple of quid
So, it's not much to look at, and yes, it's a mess.

And it hasn't worked out, but I did try my best.
But before you despair and it ruins your day
And before you dismiss it and throw it away,
Can I make a request, as I haven't a home?
I've lost all my money and I'm all alone.
And just like they say, it don't rain but it pours -
So what are my chances of Christmas at yours?

Wise Guy

Not a shepherd again Miss, I had that part last time.
This year I thought that Joseph or the donkey could be mine.
I'd be really good as Jesus Miss - I fit in that small bed.
Don't want to carry a stick and wear a tea-towel on my head.

Know what I think Miss? We should spice it up a bit.
A battle scene, some romance would make this show a hit.
No one wants nativities 2000 years behind;
Let's fill this thing with ghosts and that - the son of God won't mind.

The more I think about it Miss, we should include a fight.
We need more 007 and a bit less Silent Night.
Guns and bombs and hand grenades are what this show requires.
Explosions, downtown Bethlehem, mysterious stable fires.

Mary could get kidnapped and a shepherd has to save her -
There's this action-packed big shoot-out when she's going into
labour.
We could set it on the Death Star and I'll bring my new light saber
Think Joseph One Kenobi Miss, and I could play Darth Vader.

I know I'm taking over Miss, but I've got all the answers:
Let's have a big finale Miss, with fireworks and dancers.
I think we've got a blockbuster, so Miss let's make a start.
I'm a clever devil me, so I can play the wise man's part.

Quiet Christmas

Just gran, said mum
Oh and uncle Dan
We'll have it cosy
Spick n span
For Cheryl-Ann
And her new man
And uncle Stan
With his caravan
And then there's Jim
And cousin Tim
And Aunty Lynne
And her double chin
And violin
We'll fit her in
And her friend Keith
With the rotten teeth
He's quite fun
And his stepson'll
Want to come
Bit of a goon
He can have your room
Can't not ask Pete
From down the street
He's quite sweet
Eats no meat
But we're having goose
So he'll have to try it.
Yeah that'll do
We'll just have it quiet.

The Fridge

You won't get in there.
Don't even try.
It's full of stuff
We never needed to buy.
We bought all that Tesco's
And Spar could supply
We've emptied the Co-op,
Bled Morrisons dry.

Want to get in the fridge?
Forget it my friend.
There are packets in there
That I can't comprehend.
You can open the door,
But it's just a dead-end.
A trip to the fridge,
I won't recommend.

The turkey's in there;
It's bigger than me.
It's next to a donkey
On shelf twenty-three.
Climb over the sprouts
But there's no guarantee
That we'll see you again
'Cos you'll never get free.
You wouldn't believe
What mum's squirrelled away.
There are more things than on
Father Christmas' sleigh.
But we won't have enough
And you know what she'll say:
"Let's go to the shops
On Boxing Day."

TV Humbug

I buy the Radio Times
Every yuletide for the box.
As much a part of Christmas
As new handkerchiefs and socks.

Wallace and Gromit on the cover
Excitement in me rages.
I'm like a child on you know what,
Until I turn the pages:
An interview with Judi Dench.
A chat with Dr Who.
Behind-the-scenes at Downton Abbey
An end of year review.
Film advice with Barry Norman.
Christmas Day with Graham Norton.
Hardly fun-filled fodder
But the crossword's there to do.

Strictly Waltzing, other pleasures,
Hyacinth Bouquet.
More recycled national treasures
Drag us through the day.
A far-fetched death or love affair,
In the Rover's or Albert Square.
Casualty and Holby City -
Festive-packed cliché.
An hour of Top Gear New Year's Eve
A 'Carry On' or two.
Russell Howard's rubbish,
Another Bond to make you spew
Jamie tells us how to cook
Stephen Fry again, worst luck.
Enough to make you read a book,
Resist this hullabaloo.

So in our house, that rag is out;
I won't buy that again.
Radio Times ain't what it was:
It's £4 down the drain.
And like the losing dancer,
Takes rejection on the chin.
This year's publication's
Going strictly in the bin.

Mystery Chairs

From where do you come, O mystery chairs?
Christmas Day at around two o'clock?
Extendable family, extendable table:
Surprising enough, but how is mum able
To seat the whole sum of her flock?

Oh mystery family history chairs,
How is it you all come about?
Live you beneath coats in a room underground?
Ignored in the loft 'til December comes round?
Does Santa Clause hire you out?

Ah magic pragmatic fantastical chairs
In our midst, when we thought we had none.
Like shepherds to stable,
You come to our table
And by Boxing Day, you are gone.

Christmas Eve

One Christmas Eve an age ago,
The telly on, the fire aglow,
My mum, whilst planning lunch for ten,
Dipped in her tattered purse and then
Requested to the shop I trot
For Christmas crackers she'd forgot.

The right change in my hand squeezed tight,
I ventured into snow thick night.
Through frosty air as cold as stone
I trudged away from my warm home.
(And even by this second verse,
You'll be aware that things get worse.)

My collar raised and with full force
To Co-op I did set my course
And as the snow squeaked underfoot,
As moonlight through the fog did cut,
With icy drip upon my nose
I rushed before the shop did close.
But as I turned from street to lane
A neighbour's face in window pane
Did mouth at me that I must wait
And rest a while at garden gate.
In stringéd vest, with mug of tea
Toward their door did beckon me

My Co-op quest the neighbour sensed
And in my hand £3 dispensed
For they some cigarettes did need
(A foul addiction theirs to feed)
"Am very grateful, lad," coughed they
And I continued on my way.

Before a dozen steps I took,
Another pleading face did look
From lighted house to catch my eye
And waved a shopping list to buy:
A pint of milk, some cheddar cheese,
A loaf of bread, a tin of peas.
And sure enough, like moths to light,
Request upon request that night
Were cast my way as I did stride
On treach'rous roads where I did slide.
Not sure when I would reappear
I may be gone until new year.
Jacobs crackers, family pack;
Jammy Dodgers, string, Blu-Tak,
Tin of biscuits, After Eights,
Monkey nuts, five packs of dates,
Selection box, a leg of lamb,
Icing sugar, joint of ham,
Eleven boxes of mince pies,
(I wished the list would finalise!)
More and more change in my grips -
A bar of soap, a bag of chips!

Some washing powder, pack of pens,
Bottle of bleach, three French hens,
A loaf of bread, a Christmas pud,
Ravioli, firewood,
A roll of bin bags - extra strong,
A box of tea: lapsang souchong,
Cauliflower, spaghetti hoops.
The neighbours are all nincompoops
To spoil my Christmas Eve and send
Me out like this, their cash to spend.
While they all sit in by the fire
And Muggings gets what they require.

BAGSY THAT

So to the Holy Grail I came -
And greeted shopkeeper by name.
We gathered final Christmas treats
For lazy folk from down my street.
And with the might of a Rooney volley
I slammed the items in my trolley.

So, saddened, weighed down and alone,
I set my icy course for home.
With heavy heart and feet of clay,
Like Santa Claus without a sleigh.
But as I got to grateful neighbours,
They did reward me for my labours:
Pocket money, mincéd pie,
Chocolate bars and wink of eye.

Then finally, relieved of gifts,
I saw my house through snowy drifts.
I staggered cold to my back door
And inside feet began to thaw.
Gas fire warmth and paper chains,
And tinsel stars and board games.
With dad on sofa, mum on phone,
I tiredly slumped into my home.
Kicked off my shoes, my coat I hung.
Christmas spirit filled my lungs.
Took my hat from freezing head,
Put on pyjamas, set for bed.
But mum's voice roared like a gang of attackers:
"For God's sake lad, you've forgotten the crackers!"

Where's My Turkey?

Where's my turkey, mum?
Can anybody see it?
Is it still trapped in the oven?
Shall I go and free it?
Has anybody spotted
That bird upon my plate?
I've stared at it for ages -
Are turkeys always late?

I've shinned up my roasties
Burrowed into all my stuffing,
Upturned all the parsnips,
Can't find it; I'm not bluffing.
I've lifted all my carrots
With the help of dad and grandma
There's a frogman in my gravy
With an underwater camera.
I've searched under the table
And all around your feet;
Without a slice of Turkey,
My Christmas ain't complete.
Call off the search! I've found the thing
That I've been on about.
It was on my plate the whole time
Hid behind that brussel sprout.

What Shall We Call Him?

All night in the gloom they had shivered.
The stable, bursting with questions:
"What's this frankincense for
That they've left at the door?
Is myrrh for the feet?
Did they leave a receipt?
Has anyone got some suggestions?"

But as for a name for the baby -
Round the manger, a sea of blank faces.
They'd grappled with Gordon
And juggled with Jordan
And couldn't believe it
When Joseph said Steve
It was no way to Barry
And Harry and Gary,
But who would have thought this:
That Ken made the shortlist?
I'm sure we'd predict
A David or Benedict -
Names sent from heaven,
But maybe not Kevin
Or Graham or Des
Or Leonard or Les.
A name for the child
That wasn't too wild.
The parents were both unimpressed.
It was proving a difficult test.

Those present were scraping the barrel
For a name that suited a carol.
A name with real power
That wasn't too long,

That was nice written down,
Sounded good in a song.
A name for all time
That couldn't be shortened,
Tricky to rhyme
But sounded important.
A name of which he'd be proud.
A name that could pull a huge crowd.

A shepherd that stood 6ft 4
Bumped his head on the frame of the door.
Coming in from the night,
He misjudged the height
Which was strange as he'd been there before.

"Jesus Christ!" yelled the man with a frown,
As the blood trickled on to his gown.
"That doesn't sound bad,"
Said the son of God's dad.
"Get a pen Mary, write that one down."

Booked Up For Christmas

When the telly's on and grandad's fast asleep on top of the cat,
When her Majesty's piped down and lunch is through,
Resist the pm walk around the streets in woolly hat
And grab yourself a corner and a brew.

Then take that brand new book that Father Christmas knew you'd
like;
Now make believe the relatives have gone.
And even though aromas of your Christmas Day still linger,
Open up and breathe in chapter one.

For nothing beats the scent of untouched pages being turned.
Characters and plot that need unlocking.
So wrap yourself around it, disappear, float away -
For there is no better present in your stocking.

No Biscuits

We've got milkshake, Christmas cake,
Monkey nuts and sweets.
Parsnips, oven chips
And loads of other treats.

We've got tree chocs, selection box
Mince pies cold or hot.
All worthwhile, but I can't smile
'Cos biscuits we ain't got.

We've got fizzy pop from the shop,
Roast potatoes, toys,
Salmon, cheese, Slade CDs -
Come on feel the noise.

We've got place mats, party hats,
Crackers by the ton.
But a shocking lack of Hob-Nobs
Means my Christmas ain't no fun.

The Snowman

How can we do this to our children?
You know what I'm talking about.
5 o clock. Channel 4. Christmas Eve night.
Kids in their dressing gowns, snuggled up tight.
Mince pies on the fireplace;
Starlight everywhere.
Dim the lights; kick out the cat.
We're Walking in the Air.

Every child's favourite before they go to bed.
A snowman in the garden; magic turns his head.
He's riding on dad's motorbike,
He's lying in the freezer,
He flies above the ocean,
He's our favourite Christmas geezer.

We love him at that moment when he tries on dad's old clothes
And he makes us laugh as he picks up a banana for a nose.
When he soars off to the Arctic
Every one of us does know
That we are that little boy
As he dances in the snow.

But laughter turns to sadness and dreams turn to despair.
Like Cinderella from the ball, he's flying out of there.
And as he lands back in his garden,
We know we're going to cry.
The sky grows dim; the music slows.
He hugs his friend goodbye.

His icy pal, from hero, turns to villain in one night
In this darkened Christmas story that we wish we could rewrite.
'Cos we can't forgive the snowman
At the breaking of the day.
When the sun comes up and we all watch him
Slowly melt all away.

Starting Early

My sister starts Christmas in August.
At first, just a sprinkling of Slade.
On the beach in the sun
The plotting's begun.
By September the Christmas cake's made.

When the children start school for the new term,
Her engines are already running.
She's ransacked the town and
Bought half of Poundland -
She's nothing our kid if not cunning.

When the clocks go back she's almost ready.
The presents are under the tree.
She skips Halloween,
Bonfires, not keen.
And she's scheduled her Christmas TV.

But by Christmas Day she's almost broken:
Big job being Festive grandmaster.
But come Boxing Day
She's up and away -
Searching for Creme Eggs in ASDA.

Anything Really

Buy me some socks. A cliché I know.
But they're really the things
That make my heart sing.
Father's Day, birthdays or under the tree,
Socks from the market will satisfy me.
I know that this pressie don't scream rock n roll,
But there's nothing like socks for the soul.

Get me some hankies. All smart in a box.
When wintertime comes
And my nose starts to run,
To dip in my pocket and pull out a silk one
Satin or cotton, polyester or nylon.
Again, as a present, I can't say it rocks
But I'd love them as much as those socks.

Well, buy me some vouchers if they're a bit flash.
iTunes for music;
I'm happy to choose it.
My eighties collection could do with a lift -
Now that's what I call a number one gift.
But if that brings you out in a rash,
Forget it, just give me the cash.

Not the Pogues

What's your favourite Christmas song?
Don't say The Pogues.
We know that Irish jig they overplay.
Be handsome; be pretty
Choose a better festive ditty
When the bells are ringing out for Christmas Day.

What's your favourite Christmas song?
Wham is not the answer.
Reject that slush; don't give that song your heart.
Don't be lured in by the lair
Of George Michael's blown-dry hair.
And don't choose Chris De Burgh or Paul McCart(ney).

What's your favourite Christmas song?
Don't say Mariah.
With her uppy-downy wibbly-wobbly voice.
All you want for Christmas
Is that hit that pre-exists us.
Hang your stocking up and come on feel the noise.

What's your favourite Christmas song?
You know the one.
The greatest festive rock song ever made.
Is your stocking on the wall?
Is your Santa having a ball?
Everybody's having fun
And it's only just begun –
So here it is…
That's right, it's Bach's Christmas Oratorio
In B minor, performed by The Berlin Philharmonic.

A Shepherd's Tale

Even by the dim light of the candles in the stable,
I could see I'd made a terrible mistake.
A plethora of gifts lay by the baby in the cradle
While Joseph and his wife ate Christmas cake.

Expensive looking boxes, shiny paper, fancy ribbon
Shimmered by the manger in the cold.
A jar of oily stuff and a tub of frankincense
Leant against a massive stack of gold.

But Christmas Day's a joke round here, as all the shops are shut
And the weather where I live was turning nasty.
So I legged it to the garage and bought the baby what I could:
A pack of Mini Eggs and a pasty.

Christmas Lunch

This year, we're tired of turkey.
Our family's had a chat.
Variety is the spice of life,
So we'll be eating cat.

I know this may sound cruel
And we did have a debate.
But there can't be that much difference
Once it's sliced up on your plate.

Ok, they do make lovely pets -
Got that in their defence;
But a piece of cat is low in fat
So to me it's perfect sense.

And mum won't get so stressed this year
If Tesco's don't have any,
'Cos we've got one on the sofa
And it won't cost us a penny.

Bagsy That

A change in temperature, coal-fired air,
It was only half term but we didn't care.
For what got us through all the gloom and the fog
We're the toys in the back of the Argos catalogue.

Football could wait, forget hide and seek,
Kick the Can, Bulldog, we'll play those next week.
'Cos perched on our wall, under lamp post for ages,
We'd live out our dreams and flick through the pages.

Bagsy that bike. Bagsy that ball.
Collection of Corgi cars - bagsied them all.
Bagsy the Hot Wheels, Subbuteo set,
Lego, Scalextric, badminton net,

Buckaroo, Downfall, Connect 4 and Cluedo,
Risk - bagsied that, Frustration and Ludo.
So now in this time of technology magic,
Is it too much to ask for a time-travel gadget?
For if I could go back and relive some sights,
I'd savour the days and I'd bagsy those nights.

Brass

The brass band in the entrance of Tesco's pulls a crowd
With Jingle Bells and Winter Wonderland.
Shiny trumpets, Santa hats, a woman with a bucket.
And tinsel blu-tacked on each music stand.

We block the door and let them lead us back to yuletides past:
They remind us what this season is about.
But Christmas cheer is stopped when we remember why we're
                                                        there,
As we slide out through the door, and give 'em nowt.

Christmas Presence

Christmas cake, bah humbug.
Christmas pudding, pah!
Chocolates on the tree can go and hang.
For the highlights of the season
Aren't the presents in the morning
Or the crackers with that Marks and Spencer's bang.

It ain't the Shaun the Sheep box-set
Or the snow we never get
Or the frost that makes you glad to be alive.
They can all go to the bin
'Cos the thing that brings a grin
Is when gran and grandad pull up on the drive.

They're our frankincense and myrhh;
Even the cat begins to purr
When they park the car and shuffle through the door.
They'll sit you on their knee
And quickly drink us out of tea
Until we need to go to Tesco's for some more.

Then when he's downed our rum
And aiming not to be outdone,
Grandad tells us of the past and olden stuff.
But soon our eyes begin to drop
And then we're willing him to stop -
So roll on Boxing Day - one night's enough.

Daylight Robbery

Something out of this world this year -
More exciting than chocs or perfume.
I wanted this Christmas to be the best yet,
So I bought her a piece of the moon.

A bloke on the market with stars in his eyes
Slipped my twenty-five quid in his pocket.
He signed me a form headed: 'NASA-US'.
And then he was off like a rocket.

Wheelies

Take my Bowie records and my Star Wars DVDs;
Rip the Berghaus jacket off my back.
Cut my hair, eBay my chair and leave me on my knees
And burn my prized Adidas anorak.

Instant football access in our pockets won't placate us;
Technology ain't what us dads desire.
So eat my sweets, delete my tweets and detonate my status;
The interweb don't set our hearts on fire.

And don't head to the dads' shelves when in search of Christmas
                                                    goodies:
A ninja turtle tie won't bring us laughter.
We're not craving Marks and Spencer's when we rise on Christmas
                                                    morning -
It's those trainers with the wheels on that we're after.

As usual, the kids get all the best stuff Christmas Day,
While we're left with the jumpers and the socks.
Do you see our jealous faces when we're gathered round the tree
And those wheelie shoes are pulled out of the box?

Just imagine me and Geoff and Dave a-skating to the match
Or sliding down the aisles in ASDA shopping.
The pirouettes and spins would surely help our BMI
And work wonders for our secret body-popping.

So let us at those wheelies children! Give us dads a treat!
Rejecting our desires is just a crime.
It was us that gave you skateboards, skateparks, rollerblades
                                                    and life,
So open up your hearts it's payback time.

Party Piece

Our dad he had a party piece, each year on Christmas Day.
Teenage trials with City so to prove that he could play,
With a glass of wine in one hand and before the veg was cut,
He threw a carrot in the air and caught it on his foot.

He flicked it and he kicked it while our mum was getting dressed.
And he spun around and took a drink and bounced it off his
chest.
He knocked it with his shoulder and he tapped it with his heel
And it rotated in the air just like an orange catherine wheel.

He rolled it down his forearm and he jerked it with his hip,
And we fell around in stitches as he took another sip.
(He didn't have the skill of the all the Rooneys or Lallanas,
But I'd like to see them try it in their slippers and pyjamas).

And when we thought he'd finished and his face had turned all
red,
He took the biggest parsnip and stood it on his head.
A sprout was next for flick ups, a potato and a pea,
Then a cauli and a turnip got the treatment on his knee.

As usual, our dad had no idea when to stop -
So he chipped a cabbage in the air and took another drop.
An onion got a kicking but he wasn't finished yet,
As he lobbed it past the kettle and it landed in its net.

And when the greens were used up and he couldn't find no
more,
He searched around the kitchen as the cat flew out the door.
And just for one last magic moment from our superman -
His Christmas Day finale? Keepy-uppy with my gran

ACKNOWLEDGMENTS

My thanks to all the people (real, virtual and imagined) that have given me help and encouragement to print this book.
Merry Christmas

ABOUT THE AUTHOR

Stephen Williams is a teacher in the north of England who, to be honest, should have been marking books and planning lessons instead of writing these daft poems.

BAGSY THAT